D1308539

Junior Martial Arts
Self-Discipline

Junior Martial Arts

All Around Good Habits
Confidence
Concentration
Hand-Eye Coordination
Handling Peer Pressure
Safety
Self-Defense
Self-Discipline
Self-Esteem

Junior Martial Arts
Self-Discipline

Sara James

MASON CREST

253 4681

J
796.8
J

1
b121285911

Mason Crest
450 Parkway Drive, Suite D
Broomall, PA 19008
www.masoncrest.com

Copyright © 2014 by Mason Crest, an imprint of National Highlights, Inc. All rights reserved. No part of this publication may be reproduced or transmitted in any form or by any means, electronic or mechanical, including photocopying, recording, taping, or any information storage and retrieval system, without permission from the publisher.

Printed and bound in the United States of America.

First printing
9 8 7 6 5 4 3 2 1

Series ISBN: 978-1-4222-2731-2
ISBN: 978-1-4222-2739-8
ebook ISBN: 978-1-4222-9072-9

The Library of Congress has cataloged the
hardcopy format(s) as follows:

Library of Congress Cataloging-in-Publication Data

James, Sara.
  Self-discipline / Sara James.
    pages cm. – (Junior martial arts)
    ISBN 978-1-4222-2739-8 (hardcover) – ISBN 978-1-4222-2731-2 (series) –
ISBN 978-1-4222-9072-9 (ebook)
  1. Martial arts–Juvenile literature. 2. Self-control–Juvenile literature. I. Title.
  GV1101.35.J366 2014
  796.8–dc23
                          2013004761

Publisher's notes:
The websites mentioned in this book were active at the time of publication. The publisher is not responsible for websites that have changed their addresses or discontinued operation since the date of publication. The publisher will review and update the website addresses each time the book is reprinted.

Contents

1

MORE THAN FIGHTING

Imagine yourself as a martial artist. What are you doing? Leaping through the air? Punching bad guys? Fighting five people at once?

In real life, martial arts are a little different. They're not quite like the movies. You won't be out fighting bad guys on the street. But martial arts will teach you all sorts of cool things!

You might learn how to break a board in half with just your hand. You might learn how to flip someone to the floor.

Martial arts are about more than being strong and learning kicks. You also learn **skills** that help you deal with everyday problems. The skills you learn in martial arts can help you with friends, with your family, and at school.

Martial arts teach students to follow rules and listen to teachers. Respecting teachers is a big part of martial arts. You can't learn if you're not listening!

For example, paying close attention to other people when they talk to you is a skill. Listening helps you to be a good friend because your friends like that you listen to them.

So what sort of skills do you learn in martial arts? Lots of them! You learn **physical** skills. You learn how to balance better. You learn how to stretch your muscles. You get stronger by practicing all your martial arts moves.

Martial arts don't just make your body strong. They also help to change the way you think about things. You learn how to focus on doing one thing at a time. You learn how to treat other people with respect. You learn to feel better about who you are and what you can do.

SELF-DISCIPLINE

From the Old Days to Today

Martial arts are very old. The first martial arts were started thousands of years ago. They trained people to fight for real. Some of the first martial arts were started in Asia.

Today, we use martial arts as **self-defense**. Martial arts students don't use them to attack other people. Hurting other people is not what martial arts are about. For many people, martial arts are much more like sports than fighting.

There are hundreds of different kinds of martial arts. Martial arts come from all over the world.

Many of them come from Asia. Karate, jiu-jitsu, and aikido are from Japan. Tae-kwondo is from Korea. Muay thai is from Thailand. Kung fu (wushu) is from China.

Lots of other martial arts come from other places around the world. Capoeira and Brazilian jiu-jitsu are from Brazil in South America. Fencing and boxing started out in Europe. There are martial arts from Africa, North America, and every other corner of the globe too!

Today, you can take classes on any of these martial arts. You just have to find a school that teaches them.

Martial Arts Words

You learn special words when you study a martial art. A martial arts teacher is often called a sensei. Sensei is a Japanese word. Your martial art school is called a dojo. It's also a Japanese word. It means "place of the way."

Outside of Class

You'll learn a lot in martial arts class. It doesn't matter what kind of martial art you choose. You can use what you learn in and outside of class.

Are you having trouble in school? Martial arts can help you do better.

Martial arts can teach you how to pay attention at school. When you take a martial arts class, you learn how to **concentrate** on what you're doing. You'll have to really concentrate to learn the moves!

You also learn how to focus anywhere. So when you go to school, it's easier to pay attention to the teacher. You can concentrate on reading everything you have to. You can get through all your homework. And all those things help you do better at school.

Maybe you're not doing very well at sports. You like to play baseball and basketball. But you're not very good at them. You want to get better. Martial arts can help with that too. Maybe you're not very good at hitting the baseball when you're up to bat. Maybe you have trouble getting the basketball in the basket. You don't have very good hand-eye coordination. That means your hands and eyes don't always work together so well.

You can learn hand-eye coordination. You practice hand-eye coordination in martial arts. You have to kick and punch targets. Your teacher has you juggle and do other exercises to get better at hand-eye coordination.

And you do get better in martial arts class. You can kick the target better and better. In sports, you're doing better too. Your hand-eye coordination is better. You're hitting more baseballs. And you're getting more balls in the basket.

Self-Discipline

One other thing you learn in martial arts is self-discipline. Self-discipline means making yourself do things when you should do them, even though you don't want to do them. It means you keep doing something even if it gets hard.

Think about doing homework. You probably don't always feel like doing your homework. You get home from school. You eat a snack. Then you have to choose what to do.

Do you watch TV? Or go play outside? That's what you really want to do. You don't want to think about homework.

But you *should* do your homework. If you don't do it, you'll get a bad grade in school. And you won't learn what what you need to learn. You won't know what's going on in class.

Someone who isn't self-disciplined might choose to watch TV or play. She doesn't want to do homework. She doesn't know how to make herself do it, even though she should. She doesn't do her homework at all, so she gets a bad grade.

Someone who is self-disciplined does his homework. He knows that he should do it. He doesn't really want to, but he does it anyway. Then he can play or watch TV.

Being self-disciplined is hard. It's something that most of us have to learn.

Luckily, there are lots of ways to learn self-discipline. Taking a martial arts class is one really good way to learn more about discipline. In martial arts, you learn how to do hard things. You might not always want to do them. But you have to. And you make yourself.

Once you practice self-discipline in martial arts class, you can do it everywhere else. You can be self-disciplined at school. You can show self-discipline at home. And at sports or music practice. Self-discipline is a good skill to have!

Spotlight on Brazilian Jiu-Jitsu

Brazilian jiu-jitsu originally came from Japan. A different kind of jiu-jitsu is practiced in Japan. In the early 1900s, a jiu-jitsu teacher from Japan went to Brazil. He taught a lot of Brazilian students. Brazilian jiu-jitsu students fight a lot on the floor. There are a lot of joint locks and pinning people. There are professional jiu-jitsu fighters. But there are also schools where you can learn Brazilian jiu-jitsu, just like any other martial art.

2

SELF-DISCIPLINE & MARTIAL ARTS

Martial arts have a lot to do with self-discipline. You might not ever sit down and hear your martial arts teacher talk for a whole class about self-discipline. But you're practicing it every time you go to class.

Practicing

What do you do if you want to get better at your martial art? Practice! When you first learn a new move, you probably won't be perfect at it. It's brand new. You have to get used to doing it.

Even the very first things you learn might be hard. Learning how to stand right is one example. You might think it should be easy, but sometimes it's hard!

It takes focus and practice to earn a new belt in taekwondo. Getting a new belt can push you to work harder. And once you get your new belt, you'll feel good about what you've done.

14 SELF-DISCIPLINE

So you practice. You think about how you should be standing. Then you try and try again. After some time, you'll get it!

Once you start trying to do harder things, practicing is even more important. Trying to get that side kick just right will take a lot of work.

You might not get it right the first day you try. Or even the first week. Or the first month! Getting things right takes time.

Practicing has a lot to do with self-discipline. You would probably like to do each move perfectly the very first time. Then you can move on to harder things.

But you have to practice each move, even though you might want to skip ahead to something else. You need self-discipline to tell yourself to keep practicing.

You also might want to give up. You get upset that you can't do the move yet. Self-discipline helps you keep going, even though it's hard.

It might not be that hard to practice in class. That's what you're there for anyway. Your teacher gives you a lot of time to practice each move. She gives you tips on how to get better.

But maybe you want to get better even faster. You might want to practice at home. Instead of doing something else you'd like to do, you choose to practice martial arts. That takes a lot more self-discipline!

Moving Up

A lot of martial arts have levels. You start out at the first level. Then you move up every time you get better.

If you like martial arts, you probably want to move up levels. You don't want to stay at the first level forever. And with self-discipline, you won't!

At some point, you might want to give up. You might think your martial art is too hard. You might worry you'll never move up to the next level.

But if you have self-discipline, you'll stick with it. You'll keep trying. Every day you'll get a little better, even if you don't notice it.

It's much easier to be self-disciplined when you have a goal. Your goal is to move up a level. You want to work toward it. So you tell yourself to keep going.

You'll meet your goal soon. When you move up that level, you'll feel really good about yourself. It will be easier to keep going. It'll be easier to be self-disciplined. And then you can use your self-discipline when you keep moving up levels.

Taekwondo Levels

Taekwondo is one martial art that has a lot of levels. Each level has a different belt color. Different taekwondo schools use different colors. For the U.S. Taekwondo Academy, the first level is usually white. The next one is yellow. Then orange. You start learning kicks at this level. Next is purple. Then green, blue, and brown. After that is red and brown/red. At the top is the black belt. Just because you get a black belt doesn't mean you know everything, though. You keep learning. There are higher and higher black belt levels you can get to if you keep trying.

A black belt is a sign that a person has studied his martial art for a long time. In some martial arts, students begin to teach when they earn their black belts.

SELF-DISCIPLINE

Pushing Your Muscles

Martial arts can be hard. You're not used to doing all of the moves. Some of them might even hurt sometimes.

Even the **warm-up** exercises in martial arts can be hard. Your teacher might have you jump rope. Or run in place for a while. If you're not used to moving around much, those things could be hard.

After a martial arts class, you might be sore. You might be sweaty. You probably feel really tired.

You just have to keep your goal in mind. Why do you want to learn martial arts? Do you want to become a black belt? Do you want to learn new things? Do you want to make friends?

By remembering your goal, you can keep doing martial arts when you don't feel like it. Each day might be hard. But things will get easier and you'll get better.

You need to have self-discipline to keep going.

3

IMPROVING YOUR SELF-DISCIPLINE

Most of us could use some more self-discipline. It's really hard to tell ourselves to do something we don't really want to do.

There are lots of ways to get better at self-discipline. You can learn more self-discipline in martial arts class. And you can learn more self-discipline outside of class too.

Quitting

Quitting is the opposite of self-discipline. When you give up because something is too hard, you're quitting. If you're quitting because you just don't want to work very hard, that's not good. Maybe you don't like missing your favorite TV show because you have to go to martial arts class, even though you like the class once you get there. You shouldn't quit because of that! But there are times when it is okay to quit. If you really don't like something you're doing, you should stop doing it. If you hate going to martial arts class and don't like the people you've met in class, then maybe it's time to stop going. You should try to find something else you like to do. Maybe playing an instrument is something you'd like to do instead. Or playing a different sport. There are many activities that can help you learn self-discipline. Martial arts class is just one!

Setting Goals

The best way to practice being self-disciplined is to make goals. Goals are things you want to make happen.

In martial arts, your goals can be small or big. Small goals are learning one new move. Or not being late to class. Or making one new friend.

A bigger goal would be moving up a level in martial arts class. An even bigger goal would be getting your black belt someday. Or winning a martial arts **competition**.

To reach your goals, you have to work hard. Working to make your goals happen is one way of practicing self-discipline. You're learning self-discipline without even knowing it!

Think about what you want your goals to be. You should start with small goals. That way, you can get to them faster. Once you know you can meet your goals, you can set bigger ones.

Your goal should be really clear. Clear goals are easier to work toward. A goal that isn't clear can be harder to get to. "I want to do better in school" and "I want to be a better soccer player" aren't very clear. How will you know if you're doing better?

20   SELF-DISCIPLINE

Competitions can be a great way to push yourself to practice more and work harder. Trophies and medals are nice, but competitions are more about doing your best.

A clear goal is something like, "I will get an A on my next test." Or "I'll score a goal in my next soccer game." You'll know when you meet these goals.

You also don't want to make a goal that you can't ever meet. It's not fair to you. Don't make your goal, "I will get the highest grades in class." Or "I will get a goal in every soccer game I play." If you end up doing those things, that's great! But if you don't, you might be sad. And those are hard things to do! Most people can't do them.

Once you think of a goal, write it down. Or draw a picture. You can even put your goal up on the wall in your room. Or carry it around with you in your pocket. Being reminded of your goal will help you keep working toward it.

Now start working for your goal. This is where you practice self-discipline. It might be hard to reach your goal. You have to study to get that A. You have to practice soccer extra hard to score.

But you keep telling yourself you have to study and practice. You have to reach your goal. When you study and practice, that's self-discipline.

Don't Get Bored

Sometimes we don't like to do things because they're boring. Doing homework isn't very exciting. Practicing a ballet move over and over again to get it perfect can be boring too.

The best thing to do is make it fun! If you can turn boring things into things that are more fun, you'll want to do them. It will be easier to make yourself do them.

For example, instead of doing homework by yourself for an hour, make it more fun. Do homework with friends (just don't cheat, and make sure it gets done). Or break up your hour into two half hours. Take a walk halfway through.

Rewards

When you practice self-discipline, you're working for something in the future. Right now, you might not really want to practice an hour of martial arts every day. But it will pay off in the future.

How will it pay off? Picture how happy you'll be in the future. You will have gotten past all the hard parts. Now you're enjoying your new skills.

Maybe you want to learn how to speak Spanish. You start taking lessons after school. It's pretty hard. It's hard to remember all the words you need to know. And you can't say any of the words right yet.

When it gets too hard, imagine what will happen when you can speak Spanish. Your family is planning on taking a trip to Mexico. When you know more Spanish, you can help your family. You won't get lost because you can read signs and ask for directions.

Maybe you have a couple of friends who speak Spanish at home. It would be really cool to be able to talk to them in Spanish a little bit. So you imagine yourself talking to them and seeing how happy they are.

Thinking of yourself speaking Spanish helps you. Your self-discipline kicks in. You decide to keep learning Spanish. And you're glad you did!

Help in Class

Your martial arts teacher will help you practice self-discipline. It's something that everyone in class has to learn. And it's something your teacher has already learned and can help you with.

You might practice self-discipline in class. One day a month you might all talk about your goals. You have to come up with a goal you want to reach by the next month.

You'll get to hear everyone's goals. Some are big. Some are small. Some are things you've already done. Then you can feel good that you're self-disciplined enough to have already done so many things!

If you have questions about self-discipline, you can ask your teacher. He'll be able to tell you more about it. And give you tips on how to get better at it.

Practice Karate at Home

You can only spend a few hours a week at your karate class. If you really want to get good, you can practice at home too. You can practice stretching at home. You can practice learning the Japanese words for each move and kata (groups of moves) you know. You might read a book about karate to understand it better. And of course, you can practice your moves at home. Practice standing in front of a mirror so you can see what you're doing. Practice striking and kicking. Just don't knock anything over!

4

SELF-DISCIPLINE & YOUR LIFE

We use self-discipline all the time. It's important in martial arts classes. But it's also important in the rest of your life.

School

One place where self-discipline is really important is school. You use self-discipline all the time to do homework, take tests, and sit in class.

You might like to go to school sometimes. Maybe you really like science. It's really easy to pay attention when you're learning science. You even like doing science homework.

The kind of self-discipline that martial arts teach can help you stick to eating healthy foods. Eating right and drinking plenty of water will keep your body working at its best. That way, you can do well in martial arts class and in school!

But maybe you don't like history very much. You never want to pay attention when your teacher is talking about history. Reading history books is boring for you. You hate doing history homework.

You need self-discipline. It's still important to learn history, even if you don't like it. You have to make yourself pay attention and do your homework.

If you don't have much self-discipline, it will be really hard to learn anything about history. You'll daydream in school. And you won't do your homework. You won't have very good history grades.

If you have good self-discipline, history in school will be much easier. You still won't like it much, but you'll pay attention in school. You'll do your homework and get it over with. Then you can go do something you'd rather be doing instead.

Eating Healthy

A lot of kids think being healthy is boring. Eating healthy food isn't worth it to them. Why would you eat broccoli and carrots, they think, when you can eat french fries and candy?

Eating healthy is one of the best things you can do! You'll feel great if you eat healthy foods. You'll have a lot of energy. You might even get sick less often.

A lot of kids are overweight. They don't have healthy eating habits. Being overweight doesn't make you a bad person at all. But it can make you sick. It's better if we exercise and eat healthy.

But even though eating healthy is important, it's not always easy. You might think you don't like healthy food.

Most of us know that we should eat healthy. But we don't always do it. If you have self-discipline, you'll try to eat healthy anyway. You'll try the corn your parents make you eat at dinner. You'll eat the whole-wheat bread in your sandwich at lunch.

At first, you might think those healthy foods don't taste as good. But after you eat them a few times, you start to like them. Then you really start to like them. They start to be normal parts of your meals.

You'll feel better. Maybe you'll lose some weight. All because you had self-

discipline!

Sports, Music, and More

Self-discipline can help you out a lot in the things you do after school and on the weekends.

Do you play a sport? Do you play a musical instrument? Maybe you do art or dance. You can get better at all of those things if you have self-discipline.

In sports, you need a lot of the same self-discipline that you practice in martial arts. Sometimes things you do in sports hurt. A new exercise might make you really tired. Or you find running a mile really hard.

If you really like your sport, you'll keep going. You won't give up. You'll keep practicing even if it hurts a little. You'll keep running until you finish the mile.

Self-discipline will help you score points. And get picked to play more often. In the end, you'll be happy you stuck with it.

You need a lot of self-discipline in music too. To get better at playing an instrument, you have to practice a lot.

You might like playing your instrument. You like going to orchestra or band. And you want to be better. But it's just so hard to practice! You want to be doing other things.

If you have self-discipline, you can make yourself practice a lot. You know you have to practice to get better. So you practice a few times a week. Maybe you even try to practice every day.

Because you have self-discipline, you'll get a lot better. All that practice pays off. You have your self-discipline to thank when you sit at the front of the orchestra or get picked for an honors band.

You can use self-discipline for anything. You can use it if you dance. Or if you do art. Or if you act in plays. Self-discipline will help you be better at all these things.

Of course, self-discipline will also help you get better at martial arts. And martial arts will help you get better at being self-disciplined. It works both ways!

When you have self-discipline, you can do a lot of things better. Whether it's practicing an instrument, studying, or running a mile, self-discipline makes it easier!

Words to Know:

competition: Two or more people going against each other in a sport or activity to see who wins.

concentrate: To focus on one thing.

physical: Having to do with the body.

self-defense: Stopping another person from hurting you and making sure you're safe from danger.

skills: Things you learn that help you become a better person or live a better life.

warm-up: Stretching your muscles and getting your body moving before exercising or playing sports.

Find Out More

ONLINE

All Star Activities
www.allstaractivities.com/sports/karate/Karate-belt-system.htm

The Black Belt Club
www.scholastic.com/blackbeltclub

Kids Ask Sensei
www.asksensei.com/kids.html

IN BOOKS

Goodman, Didi. *The Kids' Karate Workbook: A Take-Home Training Guide for Young Martial Artists*. Berkeley, Cal.: Blue Snake Books, 2009.

Peterson, Susan Lynn. *Legends of the Martial Arts Masters*. North Clarendon, Ver.: Tuttle Publishing, 2003.

Wells, Garrison. *Brazilian Jiu-Jitsu: Ground-Fighting Combat*. Minneapolis, Minn.: Lerner Publishing Group, 2012.

Index

About the Author

Sara James is a writer and blogger. She writes educational books for children on a variety of topics, including health, history, and current events.

Picture Credits

www.Dreamstime.com
  Akiyoko74: p. 6, 12
  Alex099a: p. 8
  Davner: p. 14
  Hanzl49: p. 16
  Johnnychaos: p. 21
  Photoeuphoria: p. 18
  Valentyn75: p. 26
  Yuri_arcurs: p. 24